C000184305

1 MONTH OF FREE READING

at

www.ForgottenBooks.com

By purchasing this book you are eligible for one month membership to ForgottenBooks.com, giving you unlimited access to our entire collection of over 1,000,000 titles via our web site and mobile apps.

To claim your free month visit:

www.forgottenbooks.com/free918896

ISBN 978-0-265-98127-6
PIBN 10918896

This book is a reproduction of an important historical work. Forgotten Books uses
state-of-the-art technology to digitally reconstruct the work, preserving the original format
whilst repairing imperfections present in the aged copy. In rare cases, an imperfection in
the original, such as a blemish or missing page, may be replicated in our edition. We do,
however, repair the vast majority of imperfections successfully; any imperfections that
remain are intentionally left to preserve the state of such historical works.

REPORT OF ANNUAL MEETING

OF

RAMABAI ASSOCIATION

HELD MARCH 11, 1890

OF

ANNUAL MEETING

OF

Ramabai Association

HELD MARCH 11, 1890

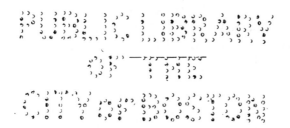

BOSTON
PRESS OF GEO. H. ELLIS, 141 FRANKLIN ST.
1890

Commonwealth of Massachusetts.

No. 3566.   *P. 30. 727*

Be it known that whereas Edward E. Hale, Phillips Brooks, George A. Gordon, Mary Hemenway, Frances Willard, Lyman Abbott, Alexander H. Rice, Pauline A. Shaw, Phebe G. Adam, Vincent Y. Bowditch, Sarah W. Whitman, Ellen F. Mason, Charles C. Shackford, Augustus Hemenway, T. Jefferson Coolidge, Jr., Antoinette P. Granger, Sarah L. Russell, Mary A. Hamilton, Mary A. Greene, Annie M. Calef, Hannah A. Adam, Minnie C. Whitman, Judith W. Andrews, have associated themselves with the intention of forming a corporation under the name of The Ramabai Association, for the purpose of assisting in the education of child-widows in India, which shall be entirely unsectarian in character, and have complied with the provisions of the Statutes of this Commonwealth in such case made and provided, as appears from the certificate of the President, Treasurer, Recording Secretary, and Trustees of said corporation, duly approved by the Commissioner of Corporations, and recorded in this office,—

Now, therefore, I, Henry B. Peirce, Secretary of the Commonwealth of Massachusetts, do hereby certify that said Edward E. Hale, Phillips Brooks, George A. Gordon, Mary Hemenway, Frances Willard, Lyman Abbott, Alexander H. Rice, Pauline A. Shaw, Phebe G. Adam, Vincent Y. Bowditch, Sarah W. Whitman, Ellen F. Mason, Charles C. Shackford, Augustus Hemenway, T. Jefferson Coolidge, Jr., Antoinette P. Granger, Sarah L. Russell, Mary A. Hamilton, Mary A. Greene, Annie M. Calef, Hannah A. Adam, Minnie C. Whitman, Judith W. Andrews, their associates and successors, are legally organized and established as and are hereby made an existing corporation, under the name of The Ramabai Association, with the powers, rights, and privileges, and subject to the limitations, duties, and restrictions which by law appertain thereto.

(SEAL.)   Witness my official signature hereunto subscribed, and the seal of the Commonwealth of Massachusetts hereunto affixed this twenty-seventh day of February in the year of our Lord one thousand eight hundred and eighty-nine.

HENRY B. PEIRCE,
Secretary of the Commonwealth.

BY-LAWS.

ARTICLE I. The members of this Association shall be such persons as shall pledge themselves to the payment of not less than one dollar per year for a period of ten years. The annual payment of one hundred dollars for ten years shall constitute a scholarship. Every member shall be entitled to vote at the annual meeting.

ART. II. The various Ramabai Circles which have been or may be formed throughout the country may become branches of this Association. Any member of such branches, pledging the payment of not less than one dollar per year for ten years, shall be a member of this Association, and shall be entitled to vote at the annual meeting.

ART. III. The officers of this Association shall consist of a President, not less than three Vice-Presidents, a Treasurer, a Recording Secretary, a Corresponding Secretary, a Board of not less than seven Trustees, an Executive Committee consisting of not less than seven persons, and an Advisory Board of three members in India. All said officers shall be elected at the annual meeting, and shall hold their offices until others are elected and qualified in their stead. Any vacancies occurring in any of the offices of this Association may be filled by the Executive Committee.

ART. IV. The Board of Trustees shall manage and control all the property and affairs of the Association.

ART. V. The annual meeting of the Association shall be held in March of each year at such time and place in Boston, Mass., as the President shall appoint.

ART. VI. The Board of Trustees shall meet semi-annually at such time and place as its Chairman shall appoint. The Executive Committee shall meet monthly at such time and place as its Chairman shall appoint. This Committee shall attend to all the business details of the Association and report to the Board of Trustees as often as such Board shall direct. It shall also make an annual report to the Association. Special meetings of the Board of Trustees or of the Executive Committee may be called by their respective Chairmen, when necessary.

ART. VII. The Advisory Board shall report to the Trustees upon such matters as may seem to them important, and upon such special matters as may be referred to them by the Association or by the Board of Trustees or by the Executive Committee.

ART. VIII. These By-Laws may be amended at the annual meeting of the Association or at any meeting called for the purpose, by a two-thirds vote of the members present and voting.

REPORT OF ANNUAL MEETING.

THE Ramabai Association held its second annual meeting in Boston, March 11, 1890. The Vice-President, Rev. Phillips Brooks, D.D., presided, opening the meeting with prayer.

ADDRESS OF REV. PHILLIPS BROOKS, D.D.

It is in the absence of our President, Dr. Hale, that there has devolved upon me the duty of presiding at this meeting. I believe that I am the commissioned bearer to this meeting of the expression of his regret that it is impossible for him to be here. He would have spoken to us from a knowledge of the work which I cannot command. I come to-day for the purpose of being instructed with regard to what has been done during the past year, and the progress of the very interesting enterprise in which our friend is engaged. The figure of Ramabai is very present with us still, and never will be forgotten by those who knew her, talked with her, and saw something of the enthusiasm with which she started upon her mission. She has carried that enthusiasm with her around the globe. It was my privilege to cross the Pacific in the steamship in which the principal of our school had crossed a few months before; and I was very deeply impressed by seeing how the officers of the steamship had been taken possession of by her enthusiasm and zeal, and how they had been swept into interest with her work. The officer of a steamship carries a great many people across the ocean, and is apt to be supremely indifferent to them; but the recollection of this lady, and of the work she had before her, and of the spirit with which she was undertaking it, was very fresh there.

We know the condition of her country, which makes her work necessary. We know the long-established social customs which have been in some sort the preservation, and in another sense the hindrance, of India. We know the new life of India, shown nowhere more clearly than in the personal experience of this lady. We know how the distant has been brought present to those who have heard her story, in this country and in other lands. And we know how the great feeling of humanity which underlies every difference of race, of custom, or of creed, has been deeply stirred as she has spoken to us. These annual occasions are of vast value, if from year to year they give us the information we need, and quicken the interest which, in the midst of the hurry and bustle of life, and the complication of a million interests pressing upon us, sometimes flags. I do, then, most earnestly bespeak your attention to the reports which will be read, and the addresses which will be made, in the hour which we shall spend together.

The Recording Secretary read the minutes of the last meeting, which were accepted.

In the absence of the Corresponding Secretary, Mrs. Russell read

MISS GRANGER'S REPORT.

At the annual meeting of the Association held in December, 1888, I reported fifty-two active Circles. To these five more were added during the following year. Among these five I count as one the Auxiliary Association of Virginia, in which clergymen of all denominations are interested, in Richmond, Norfolk, Lynchburg, and Petersburg. With their cordial support, the subject has been brought before large audiences in all these cities, and this branch association is the result. Its constitution differs slightly from that of the Circles, and its pledge is reduced to twenty-five cents, to suit the purses of Sunday-school children and others with small means. This being the case, the $150 pledged annually means a much wider interest in the work than the same sum would imply elsewhere. Last year $264 was also raised for the general fund.

Including this Virginia Auxiliary, these fifty-seven Circles, in sixteen States, Washington and Canada, with a membership of about three thousand and four hundred, have raised during the past year $4;069 for annual support, and pledge the same amount for the remaining eight years, this sum being $923 more than that pledged last year. They have also raised $631 in ten years' pledges paid in full, and $1,252 toward establishing the school, making a total of $5,952 from the Circles.

The branch association of the Pacific Coast consists of about twenty Circles.

Before going out to Bombay in September, 1889, as representative of the Executive Committee, Miss Hamlin reported $851 pledged annually, and $5,000 raised for establishing the school.

There are also many friends outside the Circles contributing toward the annual support, who are the special care of our Recording Secretary. She reports the payment for the second year of the nine scholarships, one hundred dollars each, seven of which come from as many Boston ladies; also $150 in smaller sums from scattered contributors.

During the past year a private effort has also been made by Mrs. George N. Dana, of Boston, to form clusters of ten or more persons, and to interest some of the bands of King's Daughters and Ten Times One Clubs in Ramabai's work, without demanding a ten years' pledge, which often proves a barrier to connection with a Circle. From the clusters already formed, and from personal friends, Mrs. Dana reports $111 in donations, and $75 pledged annually.

In all these branches of the work in this country the monthly letters from Ramabai and Miss Hamlin, appearing in *Lend a Hand*, have been found very interesting, and by the distribution of about four thousand leaflets and reports a knowledge of the work has been extended.

From these various sources we find that $6,017 was paid

in this past year, and is pledged annually for the support
of Ramabai's school, the Sharada Sadana, during the remain-
ing eight years of its dependence upon the Association.   This
is $1,871 more than the annual pledges of last year, and is
very encouraging, as proving an increasing interest in the
work, and confidence in Ramabai and the Association.

A. P. GRANGER,
Cor. Sec. Ramabai Ass'n.

CANANDAIGUA, N.Y., March 7, 1890.

ADDRESS OF HON. ALEXANDER H. RICE, CHAIRMAN OF THE
BOARD OF TRUSTEES.

The remarkable condition of the world in which such a
work can be started is worthy of our attention for a moment.
This is sometimes said to be a materialistic age, and no
doubt it is; but I think it is no less noble on that account.
Certainly, a materialistic age implies an age of the very high-
est intelligence among men.   For illustration, any one who
has watched the progress of the arts for the last half-century
will be impressed, I think, by the greater amount of intelligence which has been put into them.   The influence of that
intelligence is limited by no country and to no race.   The
wonderful progress of the English language, and the influence which the English-speaking race is exerting upon the
other nations of the world, however, is a most marvellous
result of this general intelligence diffused among English-
speaking people.   And the result is seen in such examples
as we have before us to-day, of the planting in the older
countries of the seed of a Christian civilization.

In closing, Mr. Rice expressed his confidence in the success of the objects which the Association has at heart, and
congratulated them on the excellent results thus far attained.

Rev. George A. Gordon was introduced, and made a brief
address.

ADDRESS OF REV. GEORGE A. GORDON.

It is touching to have the Old World turn thus to the New for aid in its efforts to regain what it has lost, and to add to its life what it has never had.

The object and motive of this work are very simple, and of this we ought never to lose sight. It is simply to bring an educated, an emancipated life, according to the Christian conception, to the degraded and suffering souls in India; to bring a life of Christian freedom and power and joy to those who are without it. We have in some measure received it, and the glory and sweetness and power that it has shed into our own souls we would share with the souls, so needy, in India. Freely we have received, freely let us give.

It seems given us to live our lives in a multiplicity of good interests. Let us accept this gladly, remembering that the greatest of specialists, though he narrow his life to the utmost, can finish nothing.

REV. MR. HAZEN, OF VERMONT.

The closing address of the afternoon was made by Rev. Mr. Hazen, of Vermont, for many years a missionary in India. He spoke with warm approval of all that had been done, and told several anecdotes to show how impossible it has hitherto been for missionaries to reach the class of women for whom Ramabai is specially interested. He also approved of the admission of women who are not widows into the school, since for many years the social customs of India will probably prevent widows from marrying. The widows will undoubtedly become the teachers of their people, but these other girls may become the mothers of the people, and the new conceptions of life which they will gain in the school will make them centres of influence.

In closing, Mr. Hazen said: "It is not necessary that there should be any turning away from Hinduism to Christianity. I speak as one who has had some little acquaintance with this matter. As the influence of Christianity is

brought to bear, it will crowd out superstition. It is most
necessary that there should be nothing to cause suspicion
and interference on the part of parents. Much has been
gained already; but it is one of our cardinal points as missionaries that men, in becoming Christians, do. not cease to
be Hindus : they stand by their own country and her customs, so far as those customs are right. Superstition will
disappear before the light of Christianity, just as false ideas
of astronomy have disappeared before the light of science.''

Voted, That the annual meeting be held in future in March,
at the call of the President, instead of in December, as
formerly.

TREASURER'S REPORT.

RECEIPTS.

Annual subscriptions for support of School,		. . . . . .	$13,357.21
"	"	General Fund, ...	10,876.83
"	"	Building Fund, ...	8,069.79
"		Scholarships, ...	3,155.00
Interest, ...			826.87
			$36,285.70

EXPENDITURES.

Salaries, ...	$4,521.00
General expenses of School, ...	2,281.00
Emergency Fund, ...	1,000.00
Papers, periodicals, Kindergarten goods for the School, . .	65.91
Ramabai's passage to India, ...	350.00
Ramabai's child's passage to India, ...	122.55
Miss Demmon's passage to India, ...	300.00
Executive Committee, ...	225.00
Printing, Stationery, Postage, Treasurer's Account Books, Incidental, ...	124.40
Balance in Bay State Trust Co., ...	27,295.84
	$36,285.70

T. JEFFERSON COOLIDGE, JR.,
Treasurer Ramabai Association.

The Treasurer called attention to a fact which illustrates the strong position of the Association. On the 1st of January, last year, the Association had $19,000 to its credit. This year, on the 1st of March, notwithstanding the expenses of the previous year, we have over $27,000 in the treasury, showing the increased interest.

CONTRIBUTIONS OF THE RAMABAI CIRCLES FOR THE YEAR ENDING
NOV. 1, 1889.

	Annual Pledges.	Pledges paid in full and Life-membership Fees.	General and Building Funds.
Baltimore, ...	$100.00	. . . . . .	. . . . . .
Brooklyn, ...	290.00	. . . . . .	$310.00
Bryn Mawr College, ...	38.00	. . . . . .	. . . . . .
Canandaigua, ...	100.00	. . . . . .	. . . . . .
" Granger Place School,	62.00	. . . . . .	. . . . . .
Chicago, ...	213.00	$47.00	25.00
Cleveland, ...	12.00	. . . . . .	. . . . . .
Concord, N.H., ...	55.00	. . . . . .	. . . . . .
Concordville, Pa., ...	31.00	. . . . . .	. . . . . .
Franklin, Del., ...	13.00	. . . . . .	. . . . . .
Geneva, ...	33.00	. . . . . .	. . . . . .
Germantown, 1st, ...	82.00	. . . . . .	. . . . . .
Germantown, 2d, ...	46.00	10.00	17.50
Gilbertsville, ...	87.00	. . . . . .	. . . . . .
Hartford, ...	107.00	. . . . . .	. . . . . .
Ithaca Cornell University, . . .	150.00	. . . . . .	. . . . . .
Indianapolis, ...	175.00	. . . . . .	. . . . . .
Jacksonville, Ill., ...	32.00	. . . . . .	. . . . . .
Jamestown, ...	. . . . . .	. . . . . .	31.00
Kansas City, ...	27.00	. . . . . .	. . . . . .
Leroy, Ingham University, . . .	63.00	. . . . . .	. . . . . .
London, Canada, ...	56.00	20.00	. . . . . .
Louisville, ...	46.00	. . . . . .	. . . . . .
Montclair, N.J., ...	50.00	. . . . . .	. . . . . .
Montreal, ...	65.00	40.00	. . . . . .
New Haven, ...	83.00	. . . . . .	17.75
New Hope, Pa., ...	9.00	. . . . . .	. . . . . .
New York City, ...	111.00	. . . . . .	280.00
" " Mrs. Brown's, . .	40.00	. . . . . .	60.00
" " Miss Merrill's, .	16.00	. . . . . .	. . . . . .

CONTRIBUTIONS OF THE RAMABAI CIRCLES FOR THE YEAR ENDING
NOV. 1, 1889.— *Continued.*

	Annual Pledges.	Pledges paid in full and Life-membership Fees.	General and Building Funds.
Niagara Falls, Canada, ...	$23.00	. . . . . .	. . . . . .
Northampton, Smith College, . .	239.00	. . . . . .	. . . . . .
Nyack, ...	50.00	$9.00	$5.50
Oswego, ...	60.00	. . . . . .	. . . . . .
Philadelphia, ...	60.00	. . . . . .	10.00
" Sahaya, ...	61.00	. . . . . .	. . . . . .
" Manorama, . . .	149.00	. . . . . .	78.00
Pawtucket, R.I., ...	6.00	10.00	25.00
Pine Bush, N.Y., ...	6.00	. . . . . .	. . . . . .
Plainfield, N.J., ...	49.00	60.00	. . . . . .
Plainville, ...	8.00	. . . . . .	5.00
Providence, Ct., ...	59.00	50.00	16.00
Quincy, Ill., ...	69.00	150.00	7.75
Richmond Association of Virginia,	138.00	. . . . . .	264.73
Roselle, N.J., ...	24.00	. . . . . .	. . . . . .
Sherwood, N.Y., ...	100.00	. . . . . .	. . . . . .
Sioux City, ...	108.00	. . . . . .	. . . . . .
Sparkill, ...	91.00	. . . . . .	. . . . . .
Springfield, ...	73.00	. . . . . .	. . . . . .
Stamford, ...	115.00	10.00	. . . . . .
St. Louis, ...	14.00	. . . . . .	. . . . . .
Toledo, Ohio, ...	13.00	. . . . . .	. . . . . .
Toronto, Canada, ...	143.00	195.00	57.12
Washington, ...	51.00	. . . . .	50.00
Wilmington, Del., ...	64.00	30.00	. . . . . .
Branch Asso. of the Pacific Coast, 20 Circles, ...	851.00	. . . . . .	5,000.00
	$4,920.00	$631.00	$6,260.35

REPORT OF EXECUTIVE COMMITTEE.

To the Members of the Ramabai Association :

The Executive Committee, in presenting their second annual report, ask you to kindly bear in mind the difficulty of reporting a work over which they can have no personal supervision and the care that must be exercised lest the statements made be not strongly colored by their own thoughts and feelings.

The first report, made in December, 1888, may be found entire in *Lend a Hand* of january, 1889. This report gave an account of Ramabai's life, ███ ██, and success in America, of her fearless travels from one end of the continent to the other, lecturing and studying, nothing escaping her keen eye and quick comprehension that could serve her great purpose. It told of the resistless power she exercised over the hearts of the people by her simple eloquence, her impassioned, pathetic appeals, which resulted in the sudden springing into existence of this Association,— an association in which men and women throughout the country, regardless of church or creed, are working together for the emancipation of millions of India's daughters from lives of ignorance and superstition, of pain and degradation. It gave an account of Ramabai's subsequent journey to the Pacific Coast, of her success there in the formation of a branch association, assisted most nobly by Miss Hamlin, and of her departure from San Francisco. The report left her bidding farewell to her friends and to the land that had grown so dear to her,— the land in which the nearness of the Father had often been revealed to her, and his love for his suffering children in the East made manifest through his children in the West. At this point, when her face, radiant with gratitude and hope, is turned homeward, the Committee again take up the thread, and will give you an account of the events that have followed. The voyage from San Francisco to Yokohama was long, tempestuous, and so fatiguing that Ramabai was obliged to rest in Japan. While there, she was a close observer of the "progressive, wide-awake Japanese women," and spoke to them several times in public on the importance of woman's education. From Japan she went to Canton, a city which seemed to her to contain " all the accumulated dirt of the world." It astonished her that people living in a place so dark and filthy could keep themselves healthy and cleanly, and produce articles of exquisite workmanship. "If I were to live a year in such a place," she writes, "I should no longer doubt my transmigration into the pig family."

The kind reception from her countrymen residing in Hong-Kong quieted a little the forebodings which naturally mingled with her hopes as she approached her own country. She was the guest of a Hindu gentleman, at whose house a social meeting was held to hear her speak of her visit in America and of her special mission. So great was the interest and enthusiasm aroused that she was urged to stay longer to create a public interest in her work. When she bade her host good-by, two enthusiastic young men accompanied her to the boat, walking one on each side of the chair in which she was carried, which they decorated with their own flowers. She wrote of this pleasing incident, "I was delighted to see the chivalrous spirit rising in the hearts of my young countrymen, who thus manifested their desire to honor woman, if only custom and circumstances would allow. I felt very proud and happy to think that the time was not far distant when my sisters would be honored by our brothers, not because they were mothers of superior beings, but because they were *women*."

Feb. 1, 1889, Ramabai touched the shores of her own country after an absence of six years. She left it a Hindu, but with a heart all aglow with a divine purpose born of the spirit of Christ; she returned a Christian, but none the less a Hindu, a true and loyal Hindu. She left it nearly penniless; she returned with the power and means to establish the school for her unfortunate sisters, which had been so many years a dream. No time was lost in going from Bombay to Poona, where she had thought to locate her school. After meeting her child Mano, from whom she had been separated three years, she sought the members of the Advisory Board appointed by this Association. Their welcome was most cordial; but the advice given greatly surprised her. They felt that the advantages of Bombay for her enterprise were superior to those of Poona, and that the school should be opened without delay, if but one pupil could be obtained. Convinced by their arguments, Ramabai returned to Bombay, consulted with prominent men whom the board had recommended, looked for a suitable school building, found one in the Choupati district, called the "Back Bay," and leased it for a year, at the rate of 135 rupees (about $45) per month.

She then met many prominent citizens of Bombay, explained to them the purpose of the institution about to be opened, told them of America's generous response to her appeals which would enable her to try her long-cherished plan, and added that she should look for the sympathy and support of her own countrymen. A temporary committee was at once chosen to co-operate with her, until one recommended by the Advisory Board of Poona could be appointed by the Association.

The school was opened with *two* pupils March 11, 1889, one month and ten days after Ramabai landed.

The opening exercises were rather novel. It was the custom for an official, dignitary, or European lady to take the lead on such occasions; and Ramabai was advised to invite Lady Reay, wife of the governor-general. But, thinking it time for the Hindu women to know how to conduct meetings, she invited Mrs. Kashibai Kanitkar to preside. She is an educated lady, who has written the life of Dr. Joshee in

Marathi. Ramabai writes that the proud and learned gentlemen of Bombay looked very resigned, and accepted good-
naturedly the honor of being presided over for the first time
by a high-caste Hindu lady. The house was adorned with
flowers and plants having symbolic meanings. A bouquet
was given to each guest, and the presiding officer, "the
heroine of the day," was adorned with a garland of flowers.
Ramabai made one of her impassioned speeches, producing
both applause and tears. Other speeches were made, all in
Marathi save one,— some eloquent, others lukewarm. The
school was thus started with the name of "Sharada
Sadana," and under far happier auspices than Ramabai, one
month before, dreamed possible. Both Ramabai and Miss
Demmon began their duties with the same earnest and brave
spirit as if there were twenty pupils instead of two.

As the government of India gives land for building pur-
poses to private schools, religious or non-religious, it has
been asked why Ràmabai did not make an application.

In April she was invited to Poona, to take part in a series
of holiday lectures. She consulted with the Board there
about this application. It was found that the English government could not give public money obtained from the
revenue for the benefit of one or two particular castes. The
missionary schools have no caste restrictions as to their
pupils. The Sharada Sadana can receive but three castes,—
Brahman, Kshatriya, Vaisya, priests, warriors, agriculturists
and merchants. If the government were willing to make an
exception of this school, a certain number of pupils, in
the beginning, would be required, and the grant would be
subject to too many conditions.

June 11, the end of the first quarter of the school, Ramabai sent to the Executive Committee a report with her accounts properly audited by a member of the Temporary
Board in Bombay. In three months her pupils had increased from two to twenty-two. Nine were living with her,
seven of whom were from the Brahman caste, and the rest
from the Vaisya community. Five were widows and three

were girls whose parents did not intend to give them in marriage until they were of proper age. The expenses of two of the pupils Ramabai paid out of her own salary. One was the child bride of a young student in the Grant Medical College. He could not pay her expenses for three years, as he had nothing but a scholarship with which to defray his own expenses. The Brooklyn Circle has recently taken her as its especial charge. The other was betrothed when but three years old; but so cruelly was she treated by her future husband's family that her father repented of his act, and secretly brought the child to Ramabai, who could not turn a deaf ear to his entreaties.

During the July vacation, Ramabai was invited to lecture in various places. She accepted, believing this to be the best means of turning public opinion in favor of the school. At Barsi, the men were so delighted that they desired her to see and speak to the women; but the women would not go to the lecture hall to hear a lecture. The men then urged her to read the Hindu Scriptures. She replied: "All right! I have, like Paul of old, to be a Jew for the Jews, and a Greek for the Greeks." Selecting a portion of one of the Puranas, she read and explained to a crowd of men and women. It was arranged that in the afternoon "this semi-religious" lecture should be delivered in the temple. "Here was the climax!" she writes. "Nobody had ever heard or seen the orthodox Hindu letting a Christian outcast enter his sacred temple! The people of Barsi not only allowed me to go into the temple, but besought me to speak and read a portion of their sacred book. I thought this was a nineteenth-century miracle!" The women were so pleased that they pressed her to stay longer. On her return to the school, she speaks most encouragingly of its progress, and quotes the indorsement of some of the missionaries who acknowledged their doubts at first of her obtaining a single high-caste woman, especially a high-caste widow. One missionary stated that she knew of many widows in Bombay who were very anxious to go to the school, and that some even cried when refused by their parents.

In September, Ramabai wrote of telling her pupils Dr. Hale's story "Ten Times One," and of their desire to do something for others. Accordingly, Ramabai translated the four mottoes, "Look up and not down," etc., into Marathi, and formed the first circle of King's Daughters in India. "Already," she writes, "I can see a change in the impish natures of my most mischievous girls. They seem to feel their responsibility. We have happy times in the evening, when all the girls come into my room and we sing together as best we can. We have no love-songs to sing, no comic bits to say; but we sing hymns, and feel quite content. You see, they do not allow women to sing; they think it a bad thing in a housewife. But we are getting unruly in this school of ours. We are going to turn the tide, and make it a good and honorable taste." The pathetic story that soon followed this account speaks eloquently for this little club of girls. A child widow of thirteen was brought to the school by her father. She was betrothed when just emerging from babyhood, and taken to live with her mother-in-law. She never knew a child's happiness; and, when her husband died, the treatment she received became cruel in the extreme. Constantly taunted with having killed her husband by some sin committed in a former existence, starved, beaten, her body often balanced through a ring suspended from the ceiling, she became prematurely old. When her father could bear the sight of her sufferings no longer and took her to Ramabai, the light had gone out of her large dark eyes, her head and shoulders were bowed as under some great burden. Ramabai's heart ached for the poor child, and she took her in. The girls, now the King's Daughters in deed as in name, also took her in. They played with her, sang to her their little songs, tried to make her forget her misery, and succeeded. Soon, strength returned to her limbs, the light to her eyes, and her whole expression changed as she felt the joy of being a free and happy child. She proves to be an intelligent and diligent pupil. The story of Gângâbai is equally sad. She was a widow at fifteen,

—an ignorant child who could neither read nor write. She was defrauded by her brother-in-law of all her jewels and the movable property of her husband to which she was entitled by the laws of that presidency. Her fine linen was replaced by the coarse garment which was to be henceforth the badge of shame. Her head was shaven and every possible indignity heaped upon her. She was forced to beg for work and food, or starve. Work she could not get. Filth, instead of food, was thrown into her little basket. Mocking, taunting words were the only answers to her piteous appeals. Three times she resolved to put an end to her miserable existence; but the fear of another incarnation into womankind restrained her. She heard of Ramabai's school and came to it, notwithstanding the curses of her people, who threatened her with excommunication, loss of caste and religion, and with all the plagues they could invoke. She came and was happy, praying night and morning that when born again it might be among the birds, and not a *woman*.

These are but two of the many sad stories that have come to the Committee, revealing to them, as they must to you, the mighty force that impelled Ramabai to consecrate her life to the redemption of child widows, the prevention of child marriage, and the uplifting of her countrywomen, and which has resulted in the founding of the Sharada Sadana.

Properly audited accounts of the expenses of the school have been received by the Committee, the last dated December 11, 1889. The expenditures from March to December, —nine months,—exclusive of Ramabai's and Miss Demmon's salaries, were 6,335 rupees, 12 annas, 1 pie ($2,111): this includes the furnishing of the Home.

There has been no extravagance in Ramabai's expenditures for the school. The small expenses that to some may have seemed useless have been incurred in conformity to the customs of the country, the non-observance of which, in the opinion of the Committee, would have been unwise. Although the Association formed at her request is but the custodian of the funds which were largely raised by her own marvellous efforts, yet, with her keen sense of honor, she fully recognizes the fact that she, no less than the officers of the Association, is responsible to the public for an economical and wise use of the money which comes from the public. Her loyalty to the Association is undoubted; and the closing words of the last report, December 11, speak her gratitude: "We are exceedingly thankful to the Almighty and to you, good friends, for helping us along in this work. All my friends here join me in thanking you for your kindness and the active interest you are taking in our widows, with a spirit of self-sacrifice. I wish you a very happy Christmas and bright New Year."

The report of 1888 spoke of the engagement of a young American teacher, Miss Demmon, and of her departure for India. She arrived a little before Ramabai, and was with her at the opening of the school. Ramabai writes in warm appreciation of her methods of teaching, the interest she rouses in the children, and of their fondness for her. Miss Demmon's own letters have never spoken of homesickness or discouragement, but always of gladness in being there, of her increasing interest in the pupils' progress, and her love for them. She has written very gratefully of the kindness of some of the zenana missionaries, who took her in when she could find no suitable boarding-place, and especially of Rev. Henry Squires, a missionary of the Church of England, in whose family she has been made to feel at home. It is to be regretted that certain complications in the housekeeping department at the opening of the school should have obliged Miss Demmon to live outside of the Home, and now that the complications are somewhat simplified that her recent illness should prevent her return at present. The Committee, in stipulating that she should be a *resident* teacher, felt that out of school hours, in the home intercourse, her love for the work to which she had consecrated herself, her tender sympathy, and her winsome manner would unconsciously exert a refining and spiritual influence over the darkened minds and repressed natures of the children. The Committee trust that arrangements will be soon made by which this plan can be carried out without detriment to the health of the teacher. It is probable that no other American teacher will be sent out to the school. The advance in female education during the six years' absence of Ramabai has been such as to make the employment of native teachers in all the departments seem possible.

During the past summer the Executive Committee became convinced that too much was being required of Ramabai; that she could not assume all the cares of the school and the home and attend to the educational and the financial matters, standing quite alone against opposition and hatred, without breaking down. They began to realize, too, that her lack of experience in teaching, organizing, and in business matters, made her work threefold the harder, and that she must have the help and sympathy of a woman of experience, judgment, and courage, or the wonderful endurance of the past three years soon would be at an end. They saw, also, that a serious mistake made at this stage of the school's existence would be fatal to its interests; and that this mistake was liable to occur through their own judgment based on partial knowledge, and through the unavoidable delay in answering appeals for advice.

Miss Sarah Dix Hamlin, of San Francisco, a woman of cultivation and refinement, of experience in teaching, organizing, and travelling, seemed peculiarly fitted for the position of adviser and helper. She was Ramabai's most loyal friend on the Pacific Coast, and was indefatigable in her efforts with Ramabai to form that branch association. With the approval of your President and the Chairman of the Trustees, the Executive Committee asked Miss Hamlin to go to India. She knew that the acceptance of the position meant social and pecuniary sacrifice; but her interest and faith in Ramabai and her work influenced her decision. She left San Francisco with the publicly expressed regrets of many of its prominent citizens, came to Boston for instructions, was elected a member of the Executive Committee, and sailed from New York in the latter part of September. Her instructions were to assist Ramabai in placing the school on a thorough business basis, to keep the Committee fully informed of the details of the school work and matters pertaining to it; and she was given authority to decide for the Committee on questions requiring immediate action, after consulting with Ramabai and the Advisory Board. It was for the purpose of obtaining satisfactory reports from her that the annual meeting was adjourned from December 13, 1889, to March 11, 1890.

Miss Hamlin's arrival in Bombay, November 8, was warmly welcomed by Ramabai and Miss Demmon. Her first impression of the school shall be given in her own words: "The house is neat, pretty, and well adapted to the needs of the school. I find here a very interesting school of twenty-five girls, including ten widows. In the house are eight widows, also seven others. Besides the fifteen pupils are the cook, who eats with them, Mano and Ramabai. The expense of the eighteen persons, inclusive of food and servants, is 135 rupees ($45) per month, or 7 rupees, 8 annas ($2.50) each. But Ramabai pays for herself, Mano, and two of the children, 30 or 32 rupees each month. In the school-room I find, from investigation thus far made, an excellent organization along the line of study. Ramabai teaches with vigor and enthusiasm, and the girls attend to her instruction with eagerness." Of Miss Demmon she writes: "Nothing is to be said of her work in school but words of praise. She is a conscientious teacher, fond of her work, devoted to Ramabai, beloved by her pupils, and most charming in her intercourse with them." Of the pupils themselves she considers the widows by far the most interesting. "They are a type of girl rarely seen. Their faces indicate that they accept their fate with resignation because they cannot help themselves; but their whole bearing is full of dignified unconsciousness of self, of quiet thoughtfulness, with a tinge of pensiveness. They show great possibilities for the future.

I love to look at them, to watch them, and feel certain that
our people would help Ramabai to many times the present
amount, could they feel the interest in these girls that I·do.
They have none of the self-confidence of the Anglo-Saxon
girls. They are wrapped up scroll upon scroll, or like the
long cell of a sea-shell, and can with difficulty be brought to
show a little of the soul within. They are quick, sensitive,
and clever, but timid. With Ramabai, however, they are
keen enough." An apt illustration of this is an incident that
occurred soon after Miss Hamlin's arrival. Ramabai rises
at three o'clock, gives an hour to correspondence, attends
to her own work, and is ready at five for the· girls. Miss
Hamlin went to her room one morning a little before the
hour. She found her ·at a table, with a Marathi Bible in
her hand, and kneeling before her, with her arms thrown
around her, sobbing bitterly, was little Godubai. The night
before she had disobeyed Ramabai; and in punishment the
good-night kiss had been omitted, which nearly broke the
child's heart. Ramabai explained that the Hindus do not
generally caress their children after infancy; and it seems
strange and delightful, especially to the poor little widows,
to receive any show of affection. At first she kissed only
her own child, then the others seemed to wish it, and now
the most orthodox come for the kiss and loving word. Miss
Hamlin may well say that the spirit of the school is very
sweet.

The first member of the Advisory Board in Bombay whom
Miss Hamlin met was Mr. Kelkar, pastor of the Brahmo-
Somaj. He was pleased to find that she had sympathy with
Hindu thought, and had not come to Americanize the school.
When he spoke of the difficulty of bringing women forward,
and the impossibility of their coming out of themselves, Miss
Hamlin merely pointed to Ramabai. "Ah," he said, "but
there is not another Ramabai in all India!"

But, with all their admiration and deference for her, never
was a woman in a more trying position. She is hated by
some of her own people because of her crusade against

superstition and caste prejudices, suspected by others because she is a Christian, and denied by Christians because
she accepts no creed. "Surely," Miss Hamlin writes, "if
any one could be tempted to forswear her Christian faith, it
is Ramabai, because of the influences around her. But she
is as unmoved as though everything were as we would have
it, knowing that, if the work be of God, it will prevail, though
all the hosts of hell were arrayed against it."

Soon after her arrival in Bombay, Miss Hamlin with
Ramabai met the Advisory Board in Poona. They found
the gentlemen much interested in the school, and ready to
give advice. They wished their own duties more clearly de-
fined by the board here, and strongly recommended the formation of an Advisory Board in Bombay. The members
were carefully selected, and their names sent to the Chairman of your Board of Trustees. The Poona board sug-
gested that an association or council be formed there, not
in any sense an official body, but one that should meet peri-
odically, report the progress of the school, and issue circu-
lars throughout the country. This course, they felt, would
prepare the people to carry on the work after the ten years
for which the Americans have pledged assistance are over.
One of the members added, "Yes; and *we* ought to be
ashamed to let it drop there."

The question of admitting to the school other than child-
widows, which is troubling some members of this Association, has been fully discussed by the Bombay and Poona
boards. While some of the gentlemen deprecate it, the
majority feel that it was the wisest and the only course
Ramabai could pursue at the opening of her school. The
two forcible reasons for keeping them in the school are: first,
the publicity it will give to the school; second, the prejudice
against widows, the feeling that they are an accursed class,
will be the sooner removed by intercourse with non-widows.
Still another reason might be urged, that the prevention of
child-marriage is an important step toward the redemption
of child-widows. The Executive Committee were asked to

act on this question : they have instructed Ramabai to keep, for the present, the non-widows that are in the school, and to admit others very cautiously, with the approval of the board, until the number of child-widows is sufficient to fill the school, when it must be for them alone. It should be said that the admittance of non-widows has added but little, if anything, to the expenses of the school. So difficult is the classification of the pupils that the same number of teachers now employed would be necessary for the widows alone. Moreover, the parents of nearly all the non-widows are able to pay a small fee.

December 25, Miss Hamlin writes : " I feel that our work here is to grow stronger, and that the outlook is even now better than it was two months ago. We have no more pupils nor any immediate promise of more ; but there is a stronger determination, a more eager enthusiasm, a more consecrated earnestness to make this work succeed."

The fifth meeting of the National Congress was held in Bombay, December 29, 1889, a graphic account of which, sent by Miss Hamlin, appeared in the *Transcript* a few weeks ago. The object of this Congress is to foster the spirit of unity among this people of divers races, tongues, and religions, and to give an opportunity for free discussion and of calling the attention of the British government to existing grievances. There was a gathering of 6,000 people,— 2,000 were delegates, with two or three women delegates received through Ramabai's influence, a fact to which the chairman referred as a matter of congratulation. The *Indian Magazine* of this month reports that upon two resolutions, one relating to marriage and the other to shaving the head and other disfigurements of the widow, Ramabai spoke with touching eloquence. She dwelt upon the injustice of depriving the widow of her property if she married again. With her usual courage, she denounced, as a wild superstition, the belief that if the widows wore their hair long it would serve to bind their husbands in hell, and asked the men how they would like to have their heads shaven because of the death of a wife! When she rose to speak, there was much crowding and pushing among the men who desired to hear her. After quiet was restored, she naïvely remarked, "It is not at all strange, my countrymen, that my voice is small, for you have never given a woman the chance to make her voice strong," and then rushed along in rapid talk, moving her audience to laughter and to tears. The *Indian Magazine* reports that these resolutions, upon which she spoke, were carried by a large majority. The resolution to request the members of that Conference to pledge themselves not to allow marriage until the bride has completed her fourteenth year was also carried by a large majority.

This action of Ramabai created an interest in the school. The house was crowded with callers. She made many friends, and received invitations to lecture in Madras and the Central Provinces. Later accounts reported her as on a lecturing tour, the subject being Education, with direct reference to child-widows. Miss Hamlin took charge of the school in her absence.

In Miss Hamlin's last letter, dated January 28, there is much anxiety expressed concerning the American newspaper accounts of the number of "converts" in the school. The Committee would caution circles and individuals against laying too much stress upon the interest which some of the pupils are showing in Christianity. They see the necessity of such caution for themselves. The beautiful pen-picture which Miss Hamlin has given of a scene she witnessed a few mornings after her arrival has touched many hearts, and more significance has been attached to it than it may have deserved. Going to Ramabai's room one morning at the hour of her morning prayers with Mano, she found eight of the older girls sitting on the lounge intently listening to the reading of the Marathi Bible. When Ramabai knelt, the girls knelt reverently with her; and she poured forth a prayer full of fervor, with an occasional "Amen." At the close each girl came forward, Ramabai said a kind word to each, and bestowed upon each a kiss, which made them very happy. When Miss Hamlin asked if this was not in violation of her pledge, she replied : " Oh, no ! these are my own private prayers. No girl is compelled to come in ; but one by one they have come of their own accord. At first, when they heard me with Mano, they peeped in the door : then one by one they ventured a little further. Occasionally one would sit, but all would leave when I knelt : now all remain." No compulsion was used nor invitation given ; it was simply the result of the "indirect influence" which Ramabai distinctly stated she should do nothing to prevent. In this she truly says she has broken no pledge. But it should be remembered that the Hindus have put such confidence in the word of Ramabai and of the American people that the school shall be strictly secular, countenancing no interference with Hindu beliefs and customs, as to unreservedly place their children under the instruction and influence of Christian teachers. The Committee feel that they but voice the sentiment of the officers of this Association in saying that even the *appearance* of breaking faith with this people should be avoided, and the utmost caution should be exercised lest Ramabai's "indirect influence" be construed into direct and proselyting influence.

The Committee are confident that neither Ramabai nor Miss Hamlin wish to destroy one faith for the building up of another, but that their purpose is to build up along the Hindu line of thought, that they may, through the people and with the people, penetrate the thick wall of prejudice and superstition. In this work, let them feel sure of the sympathy and support of their American friends. Miss Hamlin's decision to live in the school home " with natives " is a wise decision, and as brave as it is wise, because in some quarters it means social ostracism.

It is evident from certain criticisms made here and in India concerning Ramabai and the Advisory Board that several points are in danger of being forgotten. It may be well now to emphasize them. First ; that Ramabai is the founder, the head, of the Sharada Sadana; that, according to the constitution of the Association, the educational part is entirely under her control. For the financial part she is strictly accountable to the Association. Second; that as principal, teacher, and guardian, having the care of the children in the home as well as in the school, her salary is less than the salary of many *assistants* in the city schools of America. For the use of this salary she is accountable to no one. Third; that the native board was appointed by this Association, with the understanding that none but natives should belong to it. Its members were strongly indorsed by Sir William Wedderburn and Hon. Lionel Ashburner.

The Committee have pleasing proofs of England's growing interest in Ramabai's work and of its confidence in the Association. Through Miss Manning, Honourable Secretary of the Indian Association, the treasury has received £20, and £1 from a lady in Birmingham, who hoped to make it an annual contribution. From the Bishop of Bombay, Ramabai received £58.

The following extract from a letter of Professor Max Müller to Ramabai in December shows his interest in her school. He writes: "Miss Sorabji tells me how you are getting on in your work, and I am delighted to hear it. You have had a hard fight, and I suppose the battle is not yet over; but you must be pleased that you have achieved so much. I always hoped you would come back to England before you went to India, but I suppose you were anxious to begin your work. I shall be glad to hear how you are getting on. It seems to me that everything in India is moving in the right direction slowly but surely. In England, too, the feeling for India is so much improved. I promised to subscribe £5 for your Happy Home for Widows. How shall I send it to you?"

The London *Athenæum* of November 30, in a review of Ramabai's book, says: "The institution has, we understand, received the support of two of the most distinguished scholars of India, Ramakrishna Bhandarkar and Kasenath Telang. After all, the most telling argument for the scheme is the story of Ramabai's life, spent, as it has been, in the face of the severest trials. We are also glad to note that, at the recent Oriental Congress at Christiania, the Pundita's name was selected by Professor Max Müller in his published address to place with those of Ram Mohun Roy, Keshub Chunder Sen, and Nilakan Tagore as representatives of modern Indian progress."

Professor Max Müller sent to Ramabai a more recent address of his, in which he marked the following sentences: "I have never been in India; but I have known many Indians, both men and women, and I do not exaggerate when I tell you that some of them need fear no comparison with the best men and women whom it has been my good fortune to know in England, France, or Germany. Whether for unselfishness or devotion to high ideals, truthfulness, purity, and real living religion, I know no greater hero than Keshub Chunder Sen, no heroine greater than Ramabai; and I am proud to have been allowed to count both among my best friends."

The Committee have presented a long report at the risk of wearying some, because they feel it is due to the circles and individuals actively and generously interested in the school. It covers the work and events of the past fifteen months, the knowledge of which has been obtained from a weekly correspondence with Ramabai and later with Miss Hamlin. The Committee meet regularly once a month, sometimes fortnightly, to discuss and act upon the information thus received; they report and consult with the trustees at stated times; they are faithful and hopeful, realizing the great responsibility resting upon them and the consequences of one unwise step. They gratefully appreciate the confidence the Association places in them and the support that the trustees are ever ready to give.

It is with regret that they announce the resignation of one of your faithful officers, Mr. T. Jefferson Coolidge, Jr., the

Treasurer. He has been most courteous and kind in his intercourse with the Committee, and thoroughly interested in the work, in which his suggestions have been wise and helpful. Twice has he been persuaded to withdraw his resignation; but the unwillingness to allow his name to be used when it is impossible to give his time now makes the decision final. The Committee are fortunate, however, in being able to recommend a successor, both competent and experienced, who has done most of the Treasurer's work in his absence, and was recently chosen Assistant Treasurer. With the election of Mr. E. Hayward Ferry, the funds will remain in the hands of the Bay State Trust Company, 87 Boylston Street, as it is his place of business.

The Committee would utter here a word of caution against the feeling of security that the Treasurer's gratifying report may produce. Of the $27,000 in the treasury, $8,000 only belongs to the building fund; $10,000 to the general fund; $7,000 are left for the running expenses of the school. But in this sum of $7,000 are many "paid up" subscriptions for the ten years. If a deficiency in the annual income should occur at any time, it must be met by the general fund; therefore, it would not be safe, at present, to draw largely from it for building purposes. Late advices from India intimate that soon an exceptionally good opportunity for the purchase of suitable building and grounds may present itself. The Committee earnestly urge that some plan may be formed at once for raising an additional ten or fifteen thousand dollars for the building fund.

In closing their report, the Committee would remind you that the *Lend-a-Hand*, a magazine edited by your President, Dr. Hale, is the organ of the Association and contains every month some account of the school. Through it, circles and members can keep themselves well informed of the progress of the work. The office of the magazine is at 3 Hamilton Place, Boston. Price, $2 per year.

The "High Caste Hindu Woman" is still in the hands of

the Women's Temperance Publishing Association, La Salle Street, Chicago, but copies may be obtained of Messrs. Damrell & Upham, at the corner of Washington and School Streets.

Respectfully submitted,

For the Executive Committee,

` JUDITH W. ANDREWS, *Chairman.*

BOSTON, March 11, 1890.

EDITORIAL NOTES.

Ten women, including Pundita Ramabai, were délegates to the Fifth National Congress of India. Their credentials were in due form, and they were given seats on the platform. It was an unprecedented innovation, and has made a great commotion; but during the convention every reference to the lady delegates was received with cheers. *1893,*